A Tallgrass Prairie Alphabet

Claudia McGehee

University of Iowa Press

Iowa City

A BUR OAK BOOK

University of Iowa Press, Iowa City 52242
Copyright © 2004 by Claudia McGehee
All rights reserved
Printed in China
International Standard Book Number 0-87745-897-9

http://www.uiowa.edu/uiowapress

Printed with reinforced binding on acid-free paper

CIP data on file with the Library of Congress

04 05 06 07 08 C 5 4 3 2 1

To Lucy

our prairie rose

Aromatic aster

Butterfly weed

Coyote

Dickcissel

Evening primrose

Fox snake

Greater prairie-chicken

Horned lark

Ironweed

Jumping mouse

Katydid

Little bluestem

Meadow vole

Northern prairie skink

Ornate box turtle

Pasque flower

Queen of the prairie

Regal fritillary

Short-eared owl

Trout-perch

Upland sandpiper

Violet

White-tailed deer

SphinX moth

Yellow stargrass

Zizia aurea

Prairie Notes

The emerald expanse of the tallgrass prairie once covered large areas of the heartland, providing a home for a surprising variety of plants and animals. Much of this natural richness is gone forever, but remnants survive, and many people are working to preserve them and to construct new prairies. The pages of this book are dedicated to the vast prairie family, from the purple aromatic asters that bloom in the fall to the threatened ornate box turtle, which can completely enclose itself in its distinctive shell, to *Zizia aurea*, the golden alexanders that brighten the Midwest in late spring.

Aromatic aster, *Aster oblongifolius*: In the fall, after most plants have finished blooming, aromatic aster opens its flowers across the prairie. Each bushy plant has hundreds of bright purple flowers with yellow centers.

Butterfly weed, *Asclepias tuberosa*: Butterflies and other insects are attracted to butterfly weed's vibrant color and sweet-tasting nectar. The tiny flowers that make up each cluster look like little lanterns.

Coyote, *Canis latrans*: Coyotes were often called prairie wolves in pioneer days. In the evening, they sometimes yip to faraway family members.

Dickcissel, *Spiza americana*: This colorful bird, which looks like a miniature meadowlark, sings a song that sounds like its name, "Dick-dick-cissel."

Evening primrose, *Oenothera speciosa*: Evening primroses bloom at dusk and remain open throughout the night. The large flowers (*speciosa* means "showy" in Latin) attract moths and other night-flying insects.

Fox snake, *Elaphe vulpina*: These nonvenomous snakes spend hot summer days stretched out on sun-warmed rocks. They are good climbers and swimmers (fox snakes have been known to swim across rivers) but prefer to travel along the ground.

Greater prairie-chicken, *Tympanuchus cupido*: The greater prairie-chicken was once common on the prairie, but today only a small number remain. In the spring, the male fans out his fancy tail feathers, puffs up his bright orange neck sacs, and calls out a low, booming sound as part of a special courtship dance.

Horned lark, *Eremophila alpestris*: Male horned larks have two black tufts on top of their heads, like extra-large eyebrows. Unlike many other birds, horned larks prefer to nest on bare ground.

Ironweed, *Vernonia fasciculata*: Ironweed gets its name from its very tough stem. Its intense purple flowers brighten the autumn landscape.

Meadow jumping mouse, *Zapus hudsonius*: The meadow jumping mouse sleeps, or hibernates, throughout the winter in a cozy underground nest.

Gladiator katydid, *Orchelimum gladiator*: The female gladiator katydid lays her eggs on tallgrass stalks. Each katydid makes its own distinct chirping sound.

Little bluestem, *Schizachyrium scoparium*: Little bluestem is abundant in the tallgrass prairie. In the fall, its rich rusty color makes the prairie glow.

Meadow vole, *Microtus pennsylvanicus*: Meadow voles make little tunnels or runways through tall prairie grasses; they are good diggers and swimmers.

Northern prairie skink, *Eumeces septentrionalis*: This secretive skink lives in a tiny burrow; it has a long racing stripe along its brown body.

Ornate box turtle, *Terrapene ornata*: The rare ornate box turtle burrows a hole to hibernate in during the winter. This turtle has a beautiful shell, and adult males have surprising bright red eyes.

Pasque flower, *Pulsatilla patens*: When pasque flowers bloom, the tallgrass prairie spring has begun. The pasque flower blooms close to the ground, among the still-brown wintering grasses.

Queen of the prairie, *Filipendula rubra*: This plant's feathery pink flower plumes can be seen in early summer. The flowers bloom in big clusters that look a little like cotton candy.

Regal fritillary, *Speyeria idalia*: This very big butterfly sips nectar at milkweeds and thistles; its caterpillars feed on the leaves of violets. As the prairie disappears, this butterfly has a hard time finding a home.

Short-eared owl, *Asio flammeus*: Short-eared owls hunt during the daytime, as well as at night, over the wide-open prairie. You can barely see their horn-shaped tufty ears.

Trout-perch, *Percopsis omiscomaycus*: Trout-perch are usually 3 to 5 inches long. They are so named because they look like trout or perch, but they are the only member of the Persicopsidae family in North America.

Upland sandpiper, *Bartramia longicauda*: An upright bird, with a long neck and tail, the upland sandpiper sings a melodious whistling song. It once nested in incredible numbers in the tallgrass prairie.

Prairie violet, *Viola pedatifida*: The prairie violet doesn't have heart-shaped leaves, like some violets; instead, its leaves look like birds' feet (with a few extra toes).

White-tailed deer, *Odocoileus virginianus*: White-tailed deer stand tall among summer grasses and flowers. When frightened, the adult hightails out of harm's way, raising its tail like a flag to show the white underside.

Sphinx moth, *Hyles lineata*: You are most likely to see sphinx moths at dusk. Also called hawk moths, they are often confused with hummingbirds; both have similar shapes and sizes, and both hover near flowers when feeding.

Yellow stargrass, *Hypoxis hirsuta*: This plant is so delicate and tiny (about 6 inches tall in bloom) that it is easy to overlook it in the tallgrass prairie.

Zizia aurea, golden alexanders: Flat-topped flower clusters crown the tops of golden alexanders. The tiny golden-yellow flowers radiate outward from a central stem, forming a small umbrella.